Markus Bühler

The book for better websites

With pictures from
Susl 🖤

www.mach-DAS.de

Contents

START - A call for better websites (7)

What this book is all about (9)

Think from your visitor's point of view (11)

Working on your website means
working on your company (13)

PREPARATION - Think about your visitor first (15)

Forget yourself for a moment (17)

Be aware that your visitor is a real person (19)

You cannot make everyone happy (21)

Who is your visitor? (23)

Which words does your visitor use? (25)

Your visitor has basic needs that you can meet (27)

What is the goal of your visitor? (29)

Which piece of information does your visitor
need in order to achieve his goal? (31)

How does your visitor need to feel
in order to achieve his goal? (33)

II. STARTING PAGE - Your only chance (35)

Put yourself into your visitor shoes (37)

The time of your visitor is sacred and precious (39)

Get out of the web design comfort zone (41)

No „Welcome to my website" (43)

The Epicenter-Theory (45)

Your entrance gate should be simple and inviting (47)

Be helpful, useful and generous from the beginning (49)

What do you stand for? (51)

Let your customers speak for you (53)

Show yourself on video (55)

Each subpage can be a starting page (57)

III. SUBPAGES - Love at second sight (59)

Your visitor notices how much love and care
you put into your website (61)

Help your visitor to feel competent (63)

Write in an easy way (65)

No zombie texts! (67)

Feelability (69)

Interaction creates relationship (71)

Down-to-earth is touching and convincing (73)

Impulses from children's books (75)

Easy navigation rules (77)

No dead ends! (79)

Defensive web design (81)

Reflection and attraction - the benefits of a blog (83)

ABOUT - your visitor does not want to know
everything about you (85)

Create a website that offers an experience (87)

IV. BOUGHT - Win customers and fans   (89)

How often does your visitor nod when she visits your website? (91)

The little things can make all the difference (93)

Every element of your website is a transaction (95)

Make your visitor long for more (97)

The purpose of your website:
Your visitor makes progress and buys (99)

Create urgency (101)

Collect email addresses (103)

People buy results (105)

Sometimes a phone number
and a friendly smile are enough (107)

CONTACT - Remove the (last) obstacles (109)

Landing page: detours impossible (111)

Take advantage of the moment after the purchase (113)

V. EVOLUTION - Your website is thriving (115)

Revision is always a good idea (117)

Unclutter your website regularly (119)

What will your visitor remember after leaving your website? (121)

What would cause you the greatest pain
if your website went offline? (123)

Visit your website yourself - again and again (125)

Expand elements that work and that you love (127)

Use your website to solve your business bottlenecks (129)

Not every feedback is useful (131)

Experiment and test often (133)

Not everyone is able to reach the top (135)

VI EUREKA - Arrived at the top (137)

Don't lose yourself, be happy! (139)

Who are you and who are you not? Your website as a mirror (141)

Out of one single mould (143)

Industry disloyalty: Leave conventions behind (145)

A good website is like a bikini (147)

An awesome website automatically brings visitors via Google (149)

Your website is a place for your vision of paradise (151)

Empathy, the turnkey (153)

How do you act and communicate
if you don't need money or attention? (157)

Your potential million people audience (159)

Your beliefs determine what you create (161)

START

A call for better websites

What this book is all about

Websites can make a visitor happy, impress him or her lastingly and even change people's lives positively. A website can strengthen your business, provide a steady stream of new customers, and help you to optimize your business. However, most websites remain far below their potential. Way too often you encounter ego orgies, meaningless „welcome" greetings, run-of-the-mill zombie texts, and overloaded content. That's not what works for most of us. We need less ego and more courage, openness and willingness to experiment.

You will find more than ten years of website expertise in this book. I tried to identify the most helpful and inspiring thoughts on the topic and put them together in a meaningful and structured way for you. It's not about the right website system, technical tricks, or current design trends that will change over and over again every couple of weeks anyway. Rather it is about how to approach your website design in a good way. I sought to find timeless impulses that will still be up-to-date and enriching 20 years from now.

You can read the book from cover to cover and lay the foundation for a successful website. You can also choose to read that content first which fits your current questions and tasks best and implement your findings on your website straight away.

This book is telling the story of the visitor of your website: how he meets you on your website and what an enormous potential this encounter has.

Think from your visitor's point of view

Some years ago during my university psychology studies, I interviewed different company owners about their website. One of the questions was whether they themselves visit their website from time to time. The answer was almost always no. Apparently many website owners look at their website exclusively from their own perspective. That's strange because how do you want to judge whether it actually serves its purpose for the visitor?

Putting yourself at the center of your own website lowers the chance for its success. Entrepreneurs waste a lot of time and money in places where they are unnecessary while they are urgently needed at other places. The designer works hard for the perfect logo. The programmer shines with the latest technology gimmicks. Although this is a great thing in and of itself and might even bring an award in the best cases, it not only makes a website expensive but also develops it away from the visitor, and that is always the wrong direction.

So think and design your website consequently from your visitor's point of view!

The success of your website depends on real people. If you know who the person is that you meet on your website, you will be able to design this encounter consciously with intent and purpose. The easiest way to do this is to really slip into your visitor's shoes and walk with him step by step through your website.

As a nice side effect, it is very enriching for you and your company as well to really dive into that encounter with your website visitor while building your website and thinking about how to communicate what it is you offer properly.

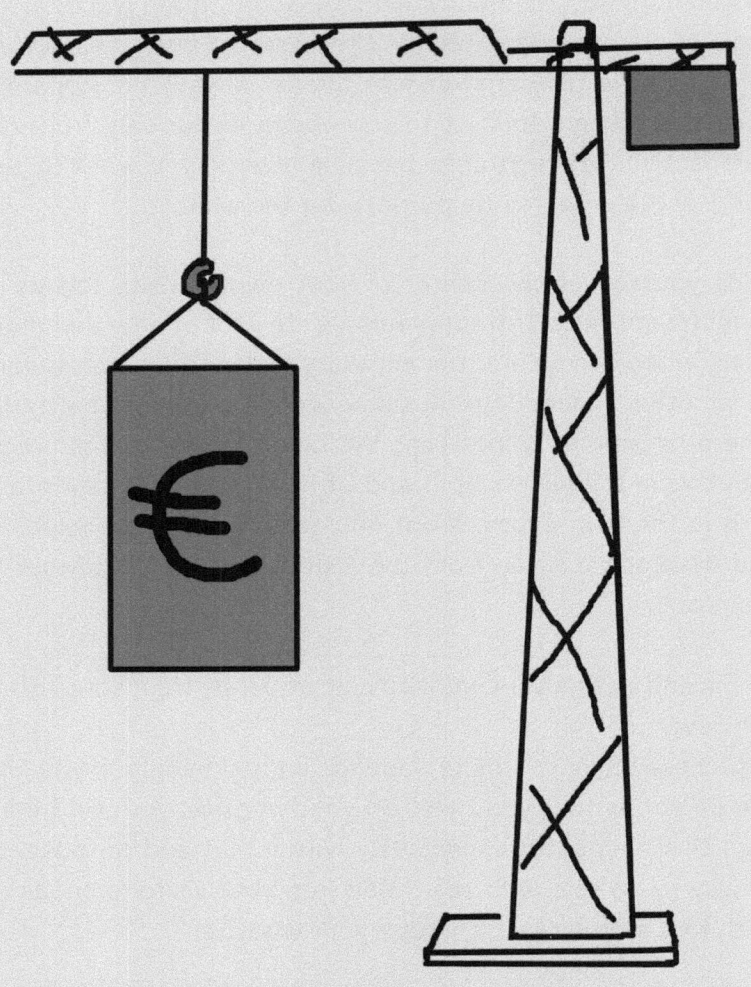

Working on your website means working on your company

Your website is the perfect place for you to reflect on your business. This great opportunity coming with building a website is often not recognized and as such remains mostly unused. In a way you look into the mirror of your company and can then identify and solve its weaknesses and bottlenecks. While your business as a whole is complex and intangible, your website makes it easier for you to perceive it, find clarity through brave choices, and take steps in the direction you want to move.

Masterminds of effective business strategies repeatedly emphasize the importance of working not only IN your business but ON your business as well. Working on the business means to broaden your view and to see your company itself as a product. In the best case, it is a product that again produces great products and services and this way generates customers and fans automatically. Small companies especially find this strategic view often difficult in the chaotic daily business.

Your website reveals a lot. Are you well-positioned? Does your vision become visible and tangible? Do you have values that you represent consistently? It helps you to find and reinvent yourself and your company. You discover what your company really is all about at its core. Now it gets exciting, because you realize that everything is possible and that you can follow your heart's desire if you want to. I wish you success in building your website, in meeting your visitors, and in evolving your company!

I.
PREPARATION

Think about your visitor first

Forget yourself for a moment

Initially don't think about yourself when you think about your website. You probably already know what you want to do with your website and what it is all about, what your offer or topic is. Now mentally go to the other side of the screen. You are someone completely different. You are your visitor, sitting at your PC and clicking through the internet. Now you come to this website. What is your first impression? How would you like to be picked up? Is there something causing joy? What information do you need to proceed? What would a great website look like? What would attract and inspire you beyond what is necessary? How does a website look or feel that you fall in love with?

Forget yourself again and again and become aware of what you are creating: an experience for your visitor. A world that he or she enters. A path that your visitor can or cannot walk along. How do you want to meet him or her? Anything but a long monologue about how great you are. Those rarely impressed us human beings. It is rather the humble people with whom we build a relationship and whom we trust because they perceive us, our needs and offer value where value is being appreciated.

You will discover that it is not so easy to think from your visitor's point of view. After all, we experience the world from our own perspective every day. You will fall into relapse, again and again, I know that from personal experience working on my own and other websites. Again and again you revolve around yourself, forgetting the visitor and asking yourself questions from your own perspective: What are my goals? Which red do I prefer? Which words do I like? What do I want to write about myself and my offer? Forget yourself for a moment. Over and over again.

Be aware that your visitor is a real person

Your visitor is a real person. Maybe he is more like you than you think. After all, you are connected by a common interest, otherwise he would not be on your site. Many website owners like to explore their statistics and that can be quite valuable. And yet, there's the danger of seeing your visitor only as a number.

You are dealing with real people here, actually, with one real person. If you realize that from the beginning, your website will become much better. You will find different words and communicate in a more personal and connecting way. That's also the reason I tend to write about "your visitor" and not "your visitors" in this book. To make it crystal clear for you.

As an exercise, I suggest you put a photo of your favorite customer on your desk. This can be a real customer, a fictional customer, or a desired customer. If you make your website for him or her, you might be able to attract more and more customers like him or her and build a stronger relationship with them.

The more concretely you imagine this, the better. Feel free to get involved with this special person and really investigate what he or she is looking for. What works for them? What doesn't? This is how you and your product or service really come to life. And there are way more customers who fit this favorite profile than you might think.

You cannot make everyone happy

Deliberately exclude people! You do not have to make your website for everyone. It is way harder to do so anyway. A wishy-washy approach that somehow pleases everyone doesn't really please anyone in the end. Make a choice about a customer, make a choice about your style. What kind of people do you want to work with? Are you looking for professional and confident clients? Do you prefer easy and open-minded people?

Think about who you want to work with and don't be afraid to exclude all other people. There will always be enough visitors you can inspire, the internet is full of people. Decide against the boring one-size-fits-all. Make a choice! Be personal, be specific. Be someone, be for someone!

If the visitors on your website are all completely different, you don't know anything about your visitor. And you lack the necessary empathy for your counterpart.

As a web designer, I have deliberately specialized in self-employed people and small businesses and work exclusively with the owners of these companies. I want to talk to the person that is in charge and most connected with the vision of the company. If a large company calls me tomorrow and wants to hire me, I say „no" in an friendly manner and without hesitation. This decision is easy for me because I know for whom I want to be here and for whom I don't.

A clear positioning with regard to your target group is also useful for the people you don't want to work with. Because these people can quickly realize that they are better off somewhere else and that saves precious time for them. And they can recommend you to a friend who might be a better fit.

Who is your visitor?

- Is your visitor a man or a woman?
- How old is your visitor?
- What is his profession?
- In which region does he live?
  In a big city, out in the countryside?

- Does he have a family?
- What is his family situation?
- Can he afford your offer?

- Does he have a faith or philosophy? If so, which one?
- What values and principles does he have?
- Is he more a person with gut instinct or rather an intellectual?

- How did he get on your website?
- Why did he end up on your website?
- What is his current situation?
- What problems does he have? What wishes?
- What images, shapes, and colors does he like?

- What words does he use?
- What is he interested in? Professionalism, sovereignty, a relaxed tone, creativity?
- What is the essence of your visitor?

Write down the answers to these and other questions as an exercise to gain extra clarity on who it is you want to work with.

search the web

Which words does your visitor use?

Words are like landscapes. Imagine us coming home from a long journey, seeing the first signs of our homes in the distance.... old feelings awaken inside. The local mountain, wide flat fields or the blossoming fruit trees in my Swab an homeland. Words trigger feelings and feelings are the most powerful force inside of a person. If we read words that we are familiar with, that are charged by our history or our hopes and wishes, we enter into a more intimate contact and relationship with the person who speaks these words. We feel that we are in the right place and have the feeling that this person is writing and talking about something that affects us directly.

Investigate into the vocabulary of your visitors. Browse through book reviews on Amazon and read what your potential visitors have to say. Look at the comments on your blog. Listen carefully to your customers. Thereby you will get closer to them and you will find out which words your audience is looking for. This way you can also make sure that more people find you through their search engine.

You can also use software tools to find out which words are searched for particularly often. Or you can find out which niche-words and phrases fit best for the target audience you want to reach. If you say the right words on your website, you will be found more easily.

What words does your ideal visitor use? Collect them. Write them down. Use them.

Your visitor has basic needs that you can meet

We all have basic needs. The need for security, for belonging, for feeling loved, comfortable, and accepted, even wanted at times. We want to get involved and make a contribution, leave a mark. There is a need for fun and fulfillment. And we want to be successful and proud of what we have achieved.

Mother Nature has given us all these needs. The great thing about these constant basic needs is that they are always relevant for every single one of your visitors. Therefore, take the needs of your visitor seriously and think about them when you are creating your content.

Our modern society offers little space for some of these fundamental needs. Many people are lonely and yearn for connection and community. Despite material abundance, many feel unfulfilled and undersupplied on a deeper emotional level. If we solve these major emotional bottlenecks, everyone will benefit.

Do you formulate in such a way that your visitor feels understood and secure? Do you offer him a place by your fire, in the midst of a loving, open, positive atmosphere?

What is the goal of your visitor?

I always used to ask my customers at the beginning of a collaboration:

„What is the goal of your website?"

But then I found a better question:

„What is the goal of your visitor?"

With this question we consistently think from the visitor's point of view. He or she has a goal. For example, your visitor may have the desire to experience something new. Or in most cases, the goal of your visitor is about solving a problem.

Even if your visitor is only looking for an important piece of information, there is a problem behind it: an information problem. For example, a person can only bake the cake if he finds a suitable recipe. Sometimes the underlying problem is completely hidden. Does your visitor want to experience something? The problem can be boredom. Or longing.

What is the problem of your visitor?
How can you help him?

Which pieces of information does your visitor need in order to achieve his goal?

The more precisely you understand which kind of information your visitor needs from you, the easier it will be for you to design useful content for your visitor.

In concrete terms: A visitor lands on your website.

Which pieces of information does he need?

- He wants to know if you can solve his problem.
  You should make this clear right on the start page.
- He wants proof of your competence.
  Give him the relevant information on your „About me" page or describe things you already made.
- He wants to know whether he can trust you.
  Quote happy customers.
- He wants to know if he can afford you or your product. Don't just formulate your offer, but also show your prices on your offer page.
- He wants to know if you are a person he likes.
  You can show yourself in a video.

Just ask your new customer what information convinced him of you to learn more about what's really important.

How does your visitor need to feel in order to achieve his goal?

When we feel good, everything works out easily. We forget time and there's no effort. With a good feeling, we naturally keep going step by step and explore what this great life has in store for us. Your visitor should feel just as good when visiting your website. And „good" has many faces. First and foremost, your visitor should like you and your company. But your website can do much more. It can inspire, enchant, surprise, help your visitor to feel taken seriously, understood, loved or alive.

What otherwise seems exhausting and slows your visitor down, is now no longer an obstacle. That's why you should consider for each subpage, each section and each element of your website: How does my visitor need to feel to move forward here? What feelings do I want to cause in my visitor? What feelings do my company and my website stand for? Everything is allowed.
Here are more suggestions for nice feelings:

Calmed, touched, moved, free, happy, honored, healthy, happy, intelligent, young, powerful, sociable, creative, motivated, curious, open, optimistic, present, privileged, calm, confident, carefree, stable, proud, brave, tolerant, perfect, alive, motivated, inspired

Make every element on your website feel right. It is in your hands.

II. STARTING PAGE

Your only chance

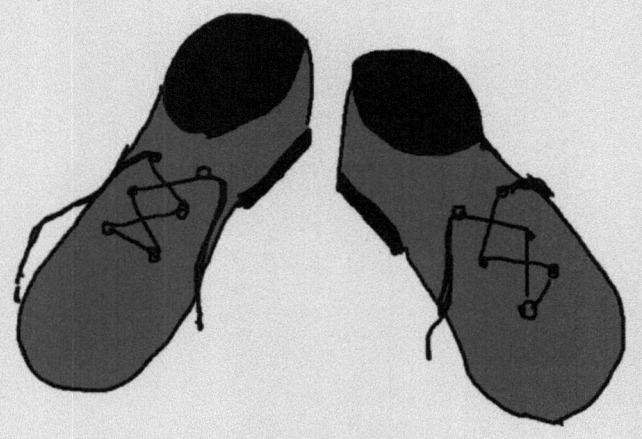

Put yourself into your visitor shoes

Many successful entrepreneurs have discovered the same holy grail for their work: In order to become really successful, it is important to ask yourself what your customer actually wants from you. What are his needs, his goals, his problems?

Put yourself into the shoes of your visitor and look at every element of your homepage as if you were seeing it for the first time. Suppose you are a tax consultant: Put yourself in the situation of someone who is looking for a tax consultant. What has just happened? You are sitting at your computer and type „tax consultant" into your Google search console and then you arrive at your page. What do you find on this page? What are your first impressions? Are you getting the information you need? Do you get a lot of information that you actually don't need at all? Which feelings does the page evoke inside of you?

It's all about not taking yourself so seriously (a nice skill in life in general) and to slip into the shoes of your visitor instead. To ask yourself the questions that arise for him or her. To see what your website does with him or her, what it means to him or her. How your website helps your visitor with his problems and wishes in the middle of this complicated world. And what he really needs, what she longs for, what you can do for him/her. You benefitting as well from this is just the icing on the cake.

The time of your visitor is sacred and precious

Time is the most valuable thing we humans have. Do not strain your visitor with long waiting periods. Be his friend by being there quickly. This will increase his sense of flow as well. Your website should load quickly, because with every additional second you'll lose more visitors.

For fast loading times, a good hosting is important and small file sizes of your pictures. Get a professional on board if your website is too slow. You should also strive to save your visitors from unnecessary headaches by communicating as simply and clearly as possible. The faster your visitor understands your message, the better.

Besides long waiting times, avoid overloaded content and confusing navigation. And also avoid automatically starting videos and sliders. Your visitor should never lose control.

Offer shortcuts on your website. Not every visitor needs all of the information you offer. Some already know you. Some follow their own feelings and interests. Some have little time. Your visitor should be able to do whatever he wants to do quickly.

You do not have to win design awards with your website. Beauty can also distract from the content, too much make-up can seem impersonal and even untrustworthy. And it can significantly increase the loading time of your website (unnecessarily).

Get out of the web design comfort zone

Most websites look similar. But don't you want to stand out from the crowd, be perceivable, special and unique? The danger is that all too often we prefer to stay in our comfort zone. We sit on the comfortable sofa and design our website in such a way that is not out of the ordinary in any way. And that is a real problem.

This is not a call for crazy and weird designs. Rather, it's about a balance between down-to-earthiness and something special. For example, you can design a few important elements different to what you are used to. You can choose extraordinary colors, extraordinary sentences, an extraordinary font. Stay authentic in everything you do. You can and should be different from others, but only if it is really you and if you feel comfortable with it.

Some conventions, on the other hand, simply make sense and therefore you should not ignore them. Your logo is in good hands if you place it in the upper left corner. It also makes sense to use words in the navigation-bar that your visitor understands: „Offers", „About us", „Contact" work just fine. But there are also elements on your website where there are many and various possibilities of an extravagant and extra appealing design. And if we want to evoke emotions or be a premium provider, we should leave the mainstream at one point or another. We usually find it hard to break conventions because we are critical of new things by nature. But you can practice this or you can just do it. Try something new and surprise your visitor and yourself. Everything is possible, you just have to allow yourself to do it. In today's world, people are generally very open and even happy about some fresh air.

No „Welcome to my website"

„Welcome to my website". You read this sentence much too often. We have all read this sentence a hundred times and therefore we don't even notice it anymore. So if someone writes „Welcome to my website", he might as well not write anything at all. What a waste in this holy place of first encounters.

Your visitor turns the corner and meets you. „Who are you?" he thinks to himself. „What is your message? Can you help me?" Surely you don't want to greet him with some profane blah-blah.

How do you want to shape the interaction with your visitor from the very first moment? With a special sentence? With a strong image? A combination of both? By briefly and clearly offering him a solution to his problem? By showing yourself from your best side?

Take care of the topics in the previous and following chapters and put them into practice, then your greeting will not only be interesting and exciting, your visitor will also feel very welcome.

With the sentence „Welcome to my website" on the other hand, you are communicating to your visitor: I have given little thought to the start of our encounter.

That is not enough.

The Epicenter-Theory

The word epicenter is one of my favorite words. I learned about it in the wonderful book REWORK by Jason Fried and David Heinemeier Hansson. There, one chapter explains how important it is to start at the core of your product or service. The job of a pizzeria is primarily to bring a good pizza on the table. You should be able to sleep well in a bed and walk well in a pair of shoes.

Bring your epicenter to the homepage! Then you will have a good start and much of what follows will fall right into place automatically and in a good and aligned way.

Like the big bang.

A good pizza attracts visitors. You make more sales and can afford a nice ambience. Then work becomes fun and the joy is transferred to the customers. You find yourself in a natural upward spiral.

What is the core of what you offer?

Write it down. Become clear about it. And then bring your epicenter to your starting page and first impression. Often people think too complicated at this point because they think everything has to be extraordinary these days. But it can and even should be simple. Your customers don't think complicated, they often want very simple and fundamental things. Show that you can deliver solid solutions.

Your entrance gate should be simple and inviting

On some websites you have to think long and hard before you even realize what's being offered. The product is unclear or way too big and extensive. Big and more is not aways attractive. With a simple entrance gate you will gain more deals and fans.

At the beginning your visitor wants to first arrive and have the feeling that he is in the right place. Especially if your offer is complex, an inviting entrance gate is very important. Be clear, be beautiful, be inviting.

Your visitor perceives how you create your entrance gate. It positions you and your offer.

Answer the following questions:

- „Which problem do you solve?"
- „What is your visitor looking for?"
- „What does your visitor desire?"
- „What does your visitor want and need?"

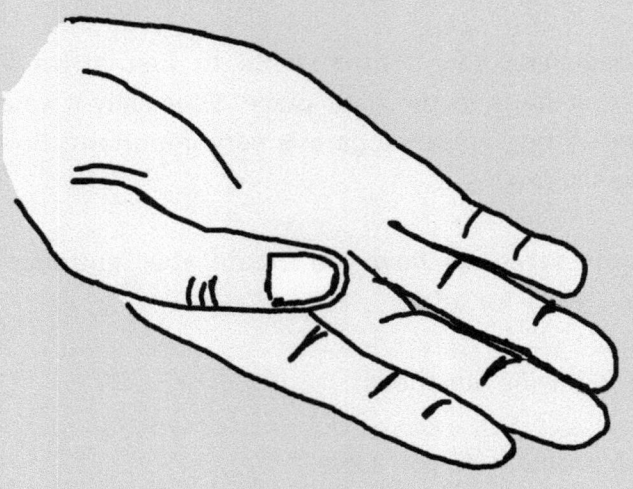

Be helpful, useful and generous from the beginning

Many websites show that the companies behind them are primarily interested in making good sales. They want to persuade you to buy something. But have you ever come across a website that immediately made you feel that its owners want your best? Where you felt picked up, appreciated, enriched and treated with care?

A school for alternative healing practitioners, for example, offers an online exam trainer on its website with which visitors can practice online free of charge. This service is extremely useful for soon-to-be alternative healing practitioners who want to pass their exam.

If you feel that you have been given a gift as a visitor, there is a good chance that you want to give something back. It also increases the probability that your visitor will come back. Give a gift with an open heart and without calculation, otherwise it is not a gift. A good blog, a useful newsletter, a great webinar. Often it's just the right words at the right moment.

You can take this opportunity to ask yourself what success means to you in the first place. Increased sales figures are nice and also an absolute goal of this book. Making your visitor happy is also a very satisfying feeling and increases your personal sense of success enormously.

What do you stand for?

A surprisingly large number of self-employed people and small companies do not stand for anything. Business as usual. They sell insurances or houses. Just the way insurances or houses are being sold everywhere. I think we should get much more involved and develop our own authentic business visions. And if we do this cleverly, we will also earn „good" money because we are unique and convincing. Then our offer can make a small but valuable difference in the world.

An example: We can sell insurances and think primarily about people and not about commissions. We can build houses with the focus on making the people who live in them happy. People primarily love (and buy) stories. So tell an interesting story to your potential customers!

When we stand up for something, everything is much more fun and has a greater impact. We no longer argue only on a level of facts but have an inner mission that gives us strength and that shines through on our website.

There is also a very practical reason why it is good: If you know what you stand for, you have much more clarity and can make decisions easier. This is a huge advantage, because you have to make a lot of decisions when building a website or a company.

Why do you do what you do? And how do you want to go on about it?

Let your customers speak for you

In this book I emphasize again and again how important it is to think from the perspective of your visitor. That is why the voices of your customers are so important and valuable. They communicate the benefits of your offer directly from the perspective of your customers. This is interesting and helpful for your visitor. That's why you should have testimonials on your homepage.

Use only real customer voices! It may be easy to invent customer testimonials, but your visitor will notice if you use real customer testimonials or not. If possible, ask for a photo in addition to a customer voice. Customer voices via videos are of course also very convincing. Also ask your customers to rate you elsewhere on the Internet where it's clear that a real person is behind it, for example on Google or Facebook.

If your customer has bought your product or service and is willing to give you a few great sentences, ask them the right questions to win useful customer testimonials that underline the special features of your offer, for example

- What did you particularly like about our collaboration?
- What was the main reason you bought my product?
- Why and to whom would you recommend me?

If you have already collected many testimonials, select the voices of the customers you would like to work with in the future. Then you will attract more people like that.

Show yourself on video

Imagine you are looking for a doctor on the Internet. You visit three websites. One of them has a video of the doctor introducing himself. This brings a lot of trust and if you like the doctor, he will probably win the race.

It took me a long time to make my first video. And many of my customers feel the same way. They find it difficult to show themselves. Maybe you like being in the spotlight, then videos are a no-brainer for you. But it could also be that you, like many other people, don't like to show yourself so much. Then it is worth overcoming yourself. Everyone likes to watch a video and gets to know you in this very easy way.

Similar to a website, a video is a great development tool for you and your company: You can perceive yourself on video and work on yourself and your appearance. Think about your video as you think about your website, and revisit the different chapters of this book.

Here are a few more practical tips:
Don't start with opening credits! Your visitor wants a useful video and you to get to the point quickly. Remember: Your visitor's time is sacred and precious. If you really want to show your logo, you can present it in the credits at the end of your video. Good sound and a good atmosphere are also very helpful and make your video more convincing.

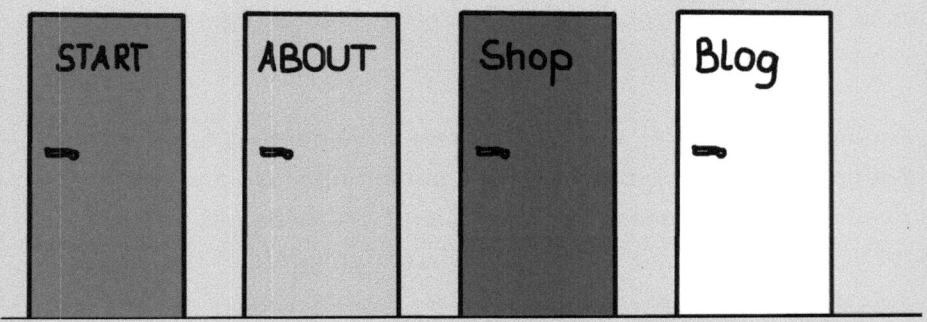

Each subpage can be a starting page

Your visitor can enter your website through different doors. The starting page is the „natural" entry point, but visitors also land directly on sub-pages, for example via links or a Google search query.

Therefore, each subpage is not only a subpage, but can also be a starting page. So we should consider each subpage not only as a step on the path, but also as a beginning. It makes sense to look at subpages in a similar way as we did with the homepage:

Put yourself into the shoes of your visitor. How does it feel to have landed directly on this subpage? How can you get to the point quickly on each subpage? Your entrance gate should be simple and inviting. Let your customers speak for you wherever possible. It can and should be clear what you stand for on every page. What are your values? What is at the epicenter of your work?

In the following section of the book we will deal with the subpages of your website or, in other words: with the next steps of your visitor.

III.
SUBPAGES

Love at second sight

Your visitor notices how much love and care you put into your website

Do you sometimes land on a website and feel that someone has carefully designed every detail with heart and mind? No spelling or formatting errors. Clear and easy to read texts. A consistent, harmonious design. This is not meant to be a plea for perfection, which never exists anyway. But it is a call for careful work and dedication to the details.

A carefully created website is attractive. It's like a place where people like to be. There, everyone feels taken seriously and treated adequately. Better create five really good subpages than ten mediocre ones. My favorite entrepreneur Jason Fried pleads for making „no debts". If you don't do the things you do in a good way right from the start, then mistakes and carelessness will fall back at you later.

Consider the structure and design of your website like a craft. A good craftsman works clean and disciplined. If he messes up his work, there are consequences. Sure, we have the opportunity to revise and improve our content again and again, and we should definitely use this opportunity. But it is most effective (and satisfying) to be concentrated on every step of the matter at hand from the very beginning.

The old saying „How you do one thing is how you do everything" helps me to bring quality into my work in less interesting activities.

Help your visitor to feel competent

My little son loves to play puzzles, but just like me, he's not very good at it. Eventually, when only a few more puzzle pieces are missing, he regularly gets shining eyes. Suddenly everything falls into place as if by itself, one glorious moment of achievement and success follows the next. Victory! He feels competent and efficient. And that is one of the best feelings a person can experience.

Steve Krug did not choose the title „Don't make me think" for his usability bestseller for nothing. Because thinking is no fun. Question marks in the head are annoying.

Create this good feeling of understanding everything right away for your visitor again and again. He will appreciate it and will happily stay on your website for a longer time. Your visitor should feel competent and you will achieve this primarily through choosing words and sentences that are very easy to understand.

Write in an easy way

Any obstacle in understanding your texts is a sales obstacle. That's why you should write your texts in a way that even a 12-year-old can understand.

Your message is clear, your offer is obvious. Your visitor is absolutely sure what he's dealing with, feels competent and in control. That's what you want! He feels good in dealing with you and your offer! Powerful, comfortable, in charge. Don't ruin it, by making him think, or feel even a slight bit of uncertainty or insecurity. Write and talk in a way that is impossible to misunderstand!

Clarity is always key.

And easy is fun!

No zombie texts!

Many texts on websites lack soul and life. You can no longer feel the people behind the texts. Anyone could have written this sterile string of words. They don't trigger any emotions or reactions inside of us other than deep boredom.

People often find it difficult to write naturally and vividly. Talking is easier. Talking is easy and natural. But in writing, everything becomes more stubborn and headstrong. Try writing the way you talk! What helps me is to imagine a friend with whom I can communicate. Write lightheartedly! At school and at university we were mostly trimmed down to formalities and top-heavy writing. You have to give it up and learn anew, but it's easier done than you might think.

Strong opinions weren't appreciated at school either. But strong opinions are important and valuable for your visitor. Take a stand! It's better to exaggerate a little than to understate. Your reader can then say YES! or NO! just as convincingly. Both times you reach him. In one case he can connect, in the other case he can clearly distance himself from your statement. Lukewarm gossip, on the other hand, does not help anyone.

If after reading your words your visitor is still the same as before, then you have not only offered him nothing of value. You have robbed him of his precious life time, this moment, seconds, in the worst case minutes void of meaning.

Write boldly, naturally and vividly!

Feelability

You have probably come across the word „usability" several times. Your website should be user-friendly. But is that enough? Shouldn't your website also have the potential to trigger emotions or feel meaningful? Feelability! I often buy „by feeling". I like the friendly saleswoman in the photo store, so I buy from her, even if it costs a few dollars more. I like to buy from the organic food store because it feels good. By now, science has proven that the majority of our decisions and behavior are based on our emotions.

We already asked ourselves the question: „What kind of emotion does your visitor need in order to reach his or her goal?" And we realized that positive feelings energize your visitor. This is extremely important and can be crucial to whether your visitor completes the purchase in the online store or not. Whether your visitor makes contact or not. Whether your visitor can easily collect all the necessary information to make a purchase or if he gives up before. So how do we create feelings? By being likeable, honest and genuine. By using big impressive pictures. By showing ourselves on video. By making our visitor smile and telling interesting stories. By whatever we can come up with when thinking from our visitors point of view in regards to the theme of feelability.

Perfection does more harm than good. People are less and less interested in glossy brochures, they want real people. We can also trigger feelings in our visitor by being useful and by offering the prospect of a solution to one of his or her problems.

Another keyword is „gamification". We can invite our visitor to interact. For example in the form of a quiz. Thus creating excitement, awaken ambition and being fun.

Interaction creates relationship

A relationship is built through interaction. For example in a conversation. If both sides can show something of themselves and thus feel a bit seen and known, automagically a relationship is forming. For example, an e-mail dialogue with your newsletter recipient. Or you offer a chat on your website. Or your visitor has the opportunity to comment on your blog. Use every opportunity to interact with your visitor. For example, via live video or in a webinar.

You can also create a relationship by making it easy for your visitor to understand you. If he sees that you don't just talk to please everyone, but that you have a style, values and a personality, then he can relate to you. When he has the feeling of getting to know you more and more, a feeling of trust develops. So dare to position yourself. Don't be afraid to be provocative, but just be casual and honest.

You just have to be the special, normal and honest person you are.

Down-to-earth is touching and convincing

People like to take themselves too seriously in business. „Look how great I am and look at my great thoughts!" That's what I communicated on my blog. I wanted to write impressive texts to position myself as an expert and innovative web designer. The change came with a friend's feedback. He told me, my texts feel artificial and that he always senses an awkward „I'm so great"-energy between the lines. And that's not very appealing.

I took this to heart and learned to write more down-to-earth. Not only does this bring better results, it also takes pressure off. I no longer have to prove something to myself and others. I can simply write down my thoughts as best I can. I am on the same level as my reader and therefore my sentences are easier to digest and take in. Just think about the people you like. Aren't they often down-to-earth people? People with whom you can connect? Sure, you're an expert in your field and you're a great person, but your quality is underlined by the fact that you don't make a big deal out of it.

You can be down-to-earth in a lot of places. With words. In design. With the logo. In the video. Avoid superlatives! „Highly valuable." „Extremely good." „Extremely beautiful." We tend to such formulations because we want to give a thought special weight. But "valuable", „good" and „beautiful" are sufficient.

Impulses from children's books

For the last four years I have been reading children's books to my two boys almost every day. Children's books are great. There is a lot of experimentation happening in there, many surprises and no rules. Everything is allowed and everything is possible. Get your old children's books from the basement or look at children's books in the bookshop or library. Especially interesting is the typography of children's books. Often there are no fixed rules for shapes, colors, language, typeface. The typography supports the content and the experience of the viewer. And this is the most important sense of good typography.

This should not be a call for you to start one wild experiment after another. Readability and professionalism are also important. Sometimes you see horrible typefaces that are an imposition on the eye and have nothing to do with creativity. Don't overdo your creative freedom! But in some places it is simply great if you break out of the usual. When you leave your comfort zone and act playfully and courageously. When you find the right measure, typography can be an impressive, surprising, curiosity awakening tool.

Just take a look at a few children's books and let yourself be inspired by the representative of your own infinite potential they are.

VS.

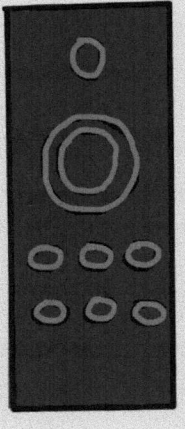

Easy navigation rules

We have two remote controls for our television at home. A conventional remote control with about forty different buttons and a modern remote control with eight. Which remote control do you think is more fun?

The small remote control is much more entertaining! I can find everything within seconds, whether I want to watch a series or open YouTube or an app. I almost only use this remote control. With the push of a button I am on the user interface, where I can select whatever it is I want to do next.

When it comes to building websites, I made the experience that it is more valuable for the users to display as few navigation points as possible - at least on the first level of your navigation bar. Furthermore, the words should be as short and on point as possible. „offers" instead of „services", „home" instead of „starting page". A lot of empty space creates clarity and your visitor gains confidence.

And you should not need more than two levels of navigation. If you need three levels, you should think about simplifying your offer or at least the content structure. On the second level it is always better to lead your visitor directly from one content-related subpage to the next without the need to use the navigation bar. Or create longer contents to save menu items. On mobile devices, your visitor prefers to „wipe" rather than click. And even on a PC, fewer clicks are an advantage.

No dead ends!

Dead ends are annoying, in real life just as much as on your website. But still you can find lots of subpages on the internet that are lacking reasonable calls for action and hence direction for the next step. Unnecessarily this is especially true for less central subpages. What do you offer your visitor when he has finished reading your blog post? Another suitable blog article? A subscription to your newsletter? Or do you let your visitor walk into the void? With nothing to turn to?

How do you lead your visitor to his next step through your world and website? With a button maybe, or a linked image or word? Is there only one next step or maybe several? Be creative and think wildly about it, but also stay practical and make sure the journey becomes clearer and richer, and not chaotic or blurred!

If you divide content into several levels, breadcrumbs are valuable. These are the link paths that are classically located above the content in the upper left corner and look like this, for example:

Home > Products > Chicken > Chicken safety vest

Breadcrumbs fulfil two important functions: They show your visitor where he is at the moment. And it is easy for your visitor to go back the way he came from within your website.

Dead ends are frustrating and prevent feelings like trust, confidence and safety. Avoid them!

Defensive web design

„With a strong offense you can win games, with a strong defense you can win titles." An old soccer saying goes something like this. Sometimes when I'm on the soccer playground, I realize that most of the players are striving to forge forward, score goals and be the king, oftentimes carelessly risking a gap in their own defense.

It's similar in web design: we want to impress, make a great video, a top design. But what about our defense?

Does this great design work on all devices? What happens if a link doesn't work and the visitor ends up on our error page? Are we prepared by offering a well designed error page that brings a smile to our visitors' face and helps him to get back to a good place on our website? Do our forms work reliably? Does everyone understand them and does the technology work so that the data is being delivered to us?

Defensive web design also means: testing, testing, testing. Over and over again. Especially with more complex functionalities like forms, online stores or member areas.

Reflection and attraction - the benefits of a blog

If you enjoy writing, I recommend a blog. A blog is extremely valuable for the following reasons:

- During the process of writing you can reflect and refine your thoughts, business, strategies, your topic and your company in a wonderful way. Regular writing and the reflecting that comes with it has a noticeable impact on the quality of your business. You become clearer and more innovative.

- Practise brings mastery. Write regularly and your writing and/or your impact in personal communication or in front of a camera will improve tremendously. People who can communicate well are almost always successful. You can practice this very well by regularly writing on your blog.

- In your blog you can pick up visitors in Google if you write about their problems and use their words. Also, good blog articles are often shared via social media.

- Your blog is a good basis of trust. Sometimes an interested visitor (=potential customer) contacts me and because of his experience with my blog posts, he feels like he knows me and my thoughts well and that means, there's already a good foundation of trust even before our first talk.

- With a blog you are building an audience. You don't have to place a ton of expensive ads anymore because your audience is already here. Whether you have a new product to offer or if you are looking for a new employee, you only have to write about it in your blog and more than enough people will be able to respond to it or share it with their friends.

- Your blog is a space of its own where many different thoughts have room that might be too many for your regular site. This way your website remains simple, lean and rich at the same time.

Can you write the best article on the internet today for a specific problem of your ideal visitor?

ABOUT - your visitor does not want to know everything about you

The „ABOUT" page is one of the most visited subpages of a website. Even if the item „About" in the navigation menu is good, because everyone understands it at first sight, you should not call the heading in the text „About me" again. That is boring and worthless. With the headline, it is always better to ask yourself the question: What is the essence of you and your company?

The web designer Ricarda Kiel suggests the following situation: A customer of yours tells another person about you and your performance. What would she say about you and your company? Customer testimonials fit very well with this. You can also tell your story, but concisely and interestingly for your visitor. A photo of you or your team is mandatory. Or alternatively a video.

The most important challenge with a good „ABOUT" page is to decide what to leave out of it. Question every sentence whether it really is of any interest for your visitor at all. A lot in your life may seem interesting to you, but is actually completely uninteresting for your visitor. Often you will find self-indulgent introduction pages, which are rambling about what great things you have already done in your life. This is annoying. Good, on the other hand, is everything that is relevant and useful for your visitor.

You should also realize that it is interesting if people don't know everything about you.

Create a website that offers an experience

Impress your visitor, move and touch him or her! Offer something valuable and interesting on every subpage of your site.

Sometimes really playful things are great, for example photos that change when you hover over them. Glowing buttons, a moving font, humorous comics like here in the book.
These are nice little experiences. You should always make sure that all effects make sense though, fit into the bigger picture and create a consistent atmosphere.

A video is always a good possibility for an experience. It creates a direct contact between your visitor and you and everything that is important to you. That's exciting! Get straight to the point, don't beat about the bush, but create something that your visitor can easily follow.

In online stores, it's great when products can be seen right away in the environment where they will later be used. Your visitor then sees not only the product, but the potential of the product. The experience of owning that product is already tangible. For example, nowadays you can buy glasses online and already combine them with a photo on the website to see how you would look with the glasses on.

What would you like to experience on your website if you were your visitor?

IV. BOUGHT

Win customers and fans

How often does your visitor nod when she visits your website?

Selling is all about collecting Yes! moments. As many and as intensive Yes!-moments as possible. When we imagine our visitor in front of the screen, a Yes! corresponds to a nod of the head.

Go through your website and perceive the „nod" potential of your content. Your visitor should nod his head regularly.

Step into relationship and have a conversation. Ask questions that your visitor can only answer with a convincing Yes! This strengthens the visitor's faith in you and your offer. You strengthen her belief that you understand her needs. Offer her something she can enthusiastically say Yes! to.

Create moments of happiness!

Remember that you cannot make everyone happy. A strong Yes! from one group of people often means that other people are determined to say No! This is not only okay, but important.

The little things can make all the difference

It's the little things that make us happy. The cup of coffee that is being brought to our bed. The postcard from a friend on vacation. The cocoa heart on your latte macchiato. Little unexpected gifts. We realize that someone really cares. And that is nice.

Do you have some icing on the cake of your website? Little things that are just nice and impressive? Special words or pictures. Or an especially nice and personal email after your visitor has subscribed to your newsletter list. Or a cheerful thank you video when someone buys your product. These little things work and distinguish your offer from others.

Which element on your website can you refine using your full attention now?

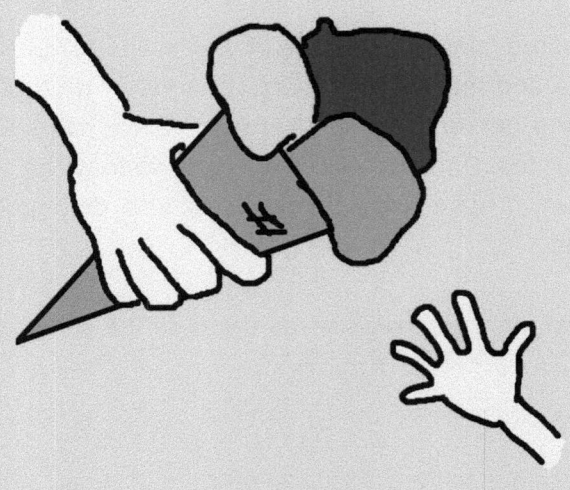

Every element of your website is a transaction

When it comes to selling we tend to only think of selling a product or a service. Perhaps we perceive it as a „sale" or at least a „success" when our visitor takes a large and measurable step, for example when she subscribes to our email list or fills out a form.

But we sell much earlier.
Because every element of our website is a transaction.

Every headline, every sentence, every picture, every video, every form. Ideally, each of these elements is being accepted and „bought".

Read every sentence on your website and think about whether the sentence is valuable and useful for your visitor. Will it get him further? Does your visitor learn something? Does it bring a positive feeling? Is it at least pleasant?

If a sentence does not bring added value, delete it. The same applies to other elements like pictures and videos. Prefer less elements with more relevant content over a lot of boring rubbish.

Make your visitor long for more

As your website visitor clicks through your website, he warms up or cools down. His buying energy grows or decreases.

Feel into your visitor and find out whether the individual elements of your website or your website as a whole are rather stimulating or narcotic, i.e. warming up, or cooling down and boring.

Ask yourself: What would inspire you? What would make you hot? Is there a way to bring this energy to your website or a specific element upon it?

Cliffhangers are often used in stories and series - a special tension or excitement at the end of an episode and you are eagerly awaiting the sequel. That works for websites, too. Every page has a goal and points to the next page. We can design the call to action for the next step in such a way that you can't wait for the next step.

A high level of buying energy is the basis for a sale, whether it is a product, a service, the subscription to a newsletter or the use of a contact form.

The purpose of your website:
Your visitor makes progress and buys

Your visitor makes many steps on your website. Some of these steps are especially big and important because they take him to the next phase. Maybe you have already dealt with online marketing before. Then you will have come across the term „conversion optimization". What is meant is the conversion of your visitor from one status to the next. You should keep these big steps in mind and measure them. What percentage of your visitors subscribe to your newsletter? How many visitors buy your product on your landing page?

The places on your website where your visitors make their big steps need special attention and special efforts. Can I make the step even more appealing? For example, with a concise button, a discount or the perfectly fitting customer voice in the right place? Can I use even better words? Can I make an inexpensive trial offer?

Make yourself aware that your visitor goes through phases.

- First he knows you, then he likes you, then he trusts you, then he buys.
- First he is a visitor, then a prospective customer, then a customer, then a fan.
- First he invests his time, then his email, then a little money, then more money, then a lot of money and love.

What incentives do you give him to move from one phase to the next?

Create urgency

Urgency works and we have the opportunity to use it authentically, honestly and to the right extent. When an online store tells me that only three units of my desired product are in stock, it sends a signal that others also like the product and it helps me to make my purchase faster.

When it comes to urgency, ask yourself: How can I make it easier for my visitor to decide on my offer? How can I shorten lengthy decision-making processes and make my offer so appealing that my visitor no longer needs to think about it?

In fact, there is always a certain degree of urgency, for example because a service provider only has a limited amount of resources, the price of a product may rise or the product may be sold out. How can you communicate the feeling that you offer something of value that is scarce in at least a broader sense?

When it comes to urgency, it is important to find the right balance. If you overdo it, you will harm your customers: Then they book offers they do not need. Or make misjudgements and believe, for example, that an offer is particularly cheap just because the „normal price" is far higher than the special offer.

Stay integer, useful and customer-oriented even when it comes to urgency, your customers will thank you in the long run.

Collect emails

A newsletter is still one of the most effective online marketing tools. You land directly in your reader's mailbox. And with every useful email that your recipient reads, you build up his trust. You have the proactive option of sending an email whenever you want, for example when you have a new product to offer.

Therefore, collect email addresses on your website from the beginning. This is not easy in times of information overload, your visitors must feel that they are receiving really valuable information with your newsletter.

So-called „content upgrades" are an effective way to do this. For example, you write a good blog article about Google optimization and offer an attractive checklist in PDF format as a „content upgrade", which your readers will only receive in exchange for their email address.

Every email address you collect is worth gold, so you should be happy about every single one. Send a newsletter even when you only have a few email addresses in your list, and don't wait until your list is big. If you do a good job, it might even be shared or recommended.

Write your newsletter regularly and consistently, for example once a week or once a month. For practise and reliability. An email list is a treasure trove because you can reach many people at once and you don't have to rely on Google or other channels that you can't really control.

People buy results

It's the result of your offer that should always be visible and tangible. Because people buy results, not services or products.

You do not sell a car, but status and pleasure. You do not sell a website, but visibility, prestige and success. You do not sell shoes, but happiness. You do not sell insurances, but security.

It is very important that you know what your visitor wants. What is the most heartfelt wish of your visitor? Talk to your customers, make a survey on your website. Think a lot about your visitor.

And then make the desired result of your product or service visible and tangible. Find out what happens when people buy your product or service.

Again, customer testimonials are great for this. Because in customer testimonials your customers automatically report the result and this will interest your visitor very much, especially if the customer testimonials come from people who are similar to your visitor.

+49(0)1525 - 3533096

Sometimes a phone number and a friendly smile are enough

Once I looked for a doctor in my city on the Internet. I ended up on a website. On the start page the doctor was shown with his team. Everybody smiled nice and likeable. Additionally the opening hours and a telephone number were shown and I could read about the things the doctor was doing and that he is also engaged in alternative healing methods besides conventional medicine.

It was immediately clear: This is the right doctor.

The website was technically hopelessly outdated, programmed sometime in the 20th century. And yet it fulfilled its purpose 100 percent, gave me all the important information in the shortest possible time. Cool.

Our visitor wants to get ahead. Sometimes that is quite simple. Then the challenge is to concentrate on what really matters to your visitor and to consistently leave out everything else.

CONTACT -
Remove the (last) obstacles

A visitor who made it to your contact page is already quite convinced of you. Now the main thing is to get rid of any possible obstacles for contacting you. Making contact is always a bit of a challenge. Some people don't like to use the phone so much. Others shy away from the effort of writing an email. So you should definitely offer different ways of making contact.

Choose the most likeable and inviting photo you can find. And as a headline a few relaxing, friendly words. You can also read the chapter „What kind of feeling does your visitor need to reach his or her goal?" in this book again and consider what feeling might be helpful for your visitor to contact you. Here are a few feelings that increase the probability of making contact:

understood, enthusiastic, free, motivated, curious, optimistic, privileged.

I discovered that a booking tool for services is worthwhile. Your visitor can book an appointment on his own and knows that you are fully available for him during this time. Offer your visitor an inviting call-to-action. That makes it easier for him or her to take the important step of contacting you, for example „Book an appointment now", „Call now" or „Write an email now".

Landing page: detours impossible

In my opinion, the term „landing page" is a misleading term. Because it is not primarily about your visitor landing on a subpage (which she does all the time), but about that one measurable goal that this page is all about. Like buying a product or subscribing to an email list.

Distractions should be avoided, that's why landing pages like to renounce the upper part of a website with logo and navigation.

That can be useful, for example, after a visitor has bought a product and placed it in her shopping cart. Now you just want her to order the product. She should no longer be distracted from the purchase. It should be as easy as possible for her to click the final button. There should no longer be difficult choices to be made.

I use the concept of landing pages very sparingly. With online stores it makes sense. Or even when filling out a complex form.

But often I decide to leave the navigation and the logo in there. I do want to build each subpage of my website in a way that my visitor always reaches one single clearly defined goal. But at the same time I also want to put the page into an overall context. Because sometimes my visitor just needs one more piece of information to really be convinced and buy.

Take advantage of the moment after the purchase

The moment your visitor converts to a new level is a very special moment. For example, he has just subscribed to your email list. Or he has bought your product. Or he has filled out and sent you some request on your contact form.

He has come closer to you, has invested, has made a commitment. At this moment he is particularly receptive. And you should treat and use this potential well.

Here are a few examples:

Your visitor buys your product. He comes to the thank you page. Here you can thank him with a nice, personal video and thus establish further trust and sympathy. You can also ask him one or two questions and find out why people decide to buy your product. Or you can ask him to share your offer on Facebook.

After the purchase is before the purchase.

V. EVOLUTION

Your website is thriving

Revision is always a good idea

„The first draft of anything is shit," said Ernest Hemingway. The first version is not much good. That's why text professionals recommend you to take yourself a lot of time to optimize a text.

Improving content again and again is exhausting, but it's worth it. With each version, your content becomes more valuable. You find more clarity, get by with one sentence where you previously needed three, find more expressive words and better headlines. It's amazing how you get better with each version. You just have to do it and you need the will to create something great and don't stop before you reach that goal. You need to start somewhere. Don't make yourself crazy about that. But then do another version, and another one. Better and better.

Sometimes it makes sense to recreate a subpage or a paragraph from scratch. In that case I recommend you to compare your new version with the previous version. That way you make sure that you haven't forgotten any important content.

Go online and be easy with a first good version of your content and don't wait too long before you publish your website, blog article or subpage. Then make sure though to keep revising your content again and again.

Unclutter your website regularly

Just like an apartment, a website also gets dirty and chaotic over time: Always new things are being added and it is difficult to part with old things.

If you want to bring new content to your website, it is important to ask yourself some questions: Do I really need this new subpage or this new paragraph? Or maybe only parts of it? Less new, less adding -> less chaos. And whenever something new comes in, it should really improve your website.

You should clean up your website regularly. Click through your website and look for phrases, images, videos and offers that you can let go of, because your business has evolved. It requires courage and clear decisions. Letting go is not easy. But anyone who has ever cleared out an apartment knows how liberating it can be. When you let go of the old, there's more space for the new. That's why clearing is a good basis for development.

Your website remains alive and the visitors who return to you feel that your company is evolving into something ever more valuable. That's attractive!

What will your visitor remember after leaving your website?

Invite people, friends and customers to visit your website. And then ask them what they remembered. This way you can discover if and why your offer might be interesting. Also try it for yourself, visit your website and ask yourself which elements and aspects of it have the potential to be remembered afterwards.

Some exciting and unforgettable examples:

- **Interesting people**
  Your visitor will remember you as a human being if you are real and authentic, have something to say or make a good presentation about your offer, for example in a video.

- **Feelings**
  Emotions are powerful. Your visitor will remember the feelings you cause within him. To do that you need to communicate things that are relevant or useful for your visitor.

- **Surprises**
  When something surprises you, your brain is very alert and therefore a stronger memory is being built. You will more easily remember your surprises. What (positively) surprising elements could you create on your website?

Create memorable moments!

What would cause you the greatest pain if your website went offline?

Sometimes you only realize the value of a website when it's offline. If you have a good hoster, your website will rarely be offline and if it is, it will only be offline for a short time.

But nevertheless ask yourself that question:
„What would hurt me most if my website went offline?"

The answer to this question might lead you directly to the epicentre of your website.

Try it and imagine for a whole day, again and again, that your website is offline. What does this trigger within you? What are the topics you are most interested in? For example, it would hurt me the most if people I'm recommended to could not view my website.

Find your answers.
And then strengthen what you miss.

Visit your website yourself – again and again

I keep telling my clients how important it is to revisit their own website many times.

My recommendation is to start right with the Google search. Google yourself, your product, your service! See how your website looks on the Google search results page. Is your presentation with title and description attractive?

Then click through your website. Read your texts, look at your pictures and videos. Test your form, make a test order in your store, log in to your member area. If something does not fit or work for you, fix it right away.

Visit your website on different devices and in different browsers. Does your website look good everywhere? Does it load quickly on mobile devices?

Make a recurring appointment in your calendar to visit your website, for example once a month.

Expand elements that work and that you love

You can see which pages, videos or blog articles resonate most for your visitor by having a look at how frequently they are being visited, commented or backlinked. You can see where your visitor stays the longest and what she buys.

Knowing this gives you hints on what kind of content you should expand and also what kind of content does not create a sense of resonance or interest. You can let go more of that.

Sometimes things work, but you don't really feel comfortable with them or you don't see any sense in them. Or they simply aren't fun. If so, think carefully about them and whether you want to continue developing these kinds of elements further or whether it is better to let go and proceed without them.

In the long run, it is most worthwhile to develop elements that work and that you love. Your intense concern with these topics will not only bring you success, but will also make you happy. They will lead you to yourself more and more.

Think also about how you can connect what you love with what is successful.

Use your website to solve your business bottlenecks

There are lots of places on your website where you can start improving. But where to begin? The idea of starting at the bottleneck might help. A bottleneck is the factor that prevents further development. For example if a plant has no water, it withers. So we just need to water it and it will continue to grow by itself. You can probably find some of these bottlenecks by just clicking through your website, for example a link that leads nowhere.

When it comes to bottlenecks, the statistics of your website are also helpful. You can see which ways your visitor goes, how long it takes him to get to where he's going and on which subpage he tends to leave your website.

Your visitor leaves your website right on the start page? Maybe he doesn't fit with your offer. Solve this by trying to bring in a more suitable visitor. Or maybe you did a bad job positioning yourself and even a suitable visitor can't see why he should book you and not some other competitor. Then you should become more visible and demonstrate your solution to a problem in a way that your visitor understands right away. Your blog articles are not being read and shared? Then you're missing the point and should first find out what your visitor wants to read.

To solve bottlenecks means to build bridges for your visitor. By doing so you give yourself and your company the opportunity to grow.

Not every feedback is useful

While you are building your website and especially when you go online with your website, you might get a lot of feedback from many different people. Over the last few years I experienced many times that feedback can sometimes be counterproductive. Feedback can provide important insights, the view from outside is fresh and unbiased. But feedback also has the potential to unsettle you and throw you into chaos.

Here are my tips on how to choose the right sources for your feedback and get helpful feedback:

- **Ask one of your ideal customers**
  The feedback of your favorite customers is highly relevant, while opinions of people who might tick completely differently than your target group are irrelevant and worthless.

- **Focused feedback**
  Formulate your questions as precisely as possible. Do not ask „Do you like my website?", but concentrate on a concrete question that you are unsure about and that your counterpart assesses competently. For example, you could ask a designer: „What do you think of my colors?" or you could ask a friend: „Do the texts suit me? Is this me?"

- **Less is more**
  Better two competent feedbacks than any ten. Take enough time to choose the right people and ask the right questions.

Experiment and test often

Yay, experimenting is great!

And as in life, experiments on websites are very valuable. Without them, there will be no progress. Sometimes you should be brave and try different things until you discover what works and gain the long awaited success. It often takes many attempts until you will find an online strategy that produces the results you want.

Tests are also very important. In online marketing, you often don't know what works best. Tests are more objective than your own thoughts and estimates. The simplest form of testing is live testing with a real person who walks through your website and gives you relevant feedback in the moment of experience. Sometimes you learn most by simply observing him or her and how he or she navigates through your page. You already know how important it is to select suitable people here. You can find websites that offer such tests or you can do a so-called A/B test: You run two versions of an item, for example two different headlines or two different pictures, sending some people to version A and others to version B. Then you see which version is more logical or appealing for your visitor, which version he will click more likely or where he stays longer.

Testing a website is one of the more advanced activities in the development of a website and only valuable once you have generated a continuous stream of visitors. However, if you test regularly, your website will benefit enormously because you will learn something new with each test.

Not everyone is able to reach the top

If you don't invest time, thought and resources in your website, your website will always remain just one out of many. Maybe you will succeed, maybe not. In any case, you won't be standing on Mount Olympus and you won't experience the joy that comes from putting your heart and soul into your website. It is a rewarding and satisfying process with all the puzzle pieces fitting together more and more merging into a coherent whole.

It makes all the difference whether you spend five minutes thinking about your visitor or a day every week. Whether you just think about it or actually write your thoughts down. Whether you revise a headline or a text three times or ten times. A website is created quickly, but a really good website takes time and effort.

So don't prepare yourself for a happy little walk, but rather for a marathon or a challenging mountain climb (and an awesome view the higher you get!). Basically a website will never be finished. Your business will change with you and your customers will change as well. Get rid of the idea of getting done and enjoyingly relax into the eternal process. There is no such thing as „perfect". Anyway, your website can always become ever clearer, more alive and more authentic.

You think your website is great already?
Better get back to work.

VI. EUREKA

Arrived at the top

Don't lose yourself, be happy!

This book told you to think from your visitor's point of view and even forget yourself from time to time. But that does not mean you should lose yourself in the process. Quite the opposite. By widening your view and heart and thinking and acting with compassion, your self will grow bigger and you will become more successful.

You will include the feelings, the worries, the needs and the hopes of your visitor into your own considerations. And you will create an encounter that enriches your visitor - just as you welcome a guest into your home. You think about how to make the arrival perfect and which areas of your house might be interesting for him and how you would like to arrange it all best. Is there music? Are there some snacks?

If you create a happy visitor who enjoys and accepts your house, you will be happy too. Be aware that it is your house that you are passionately working on. A house where you feel comfortable and that shows who you are. You become more and more yourself.

What makes you happy?
Which people do you like to make happy most? And how?

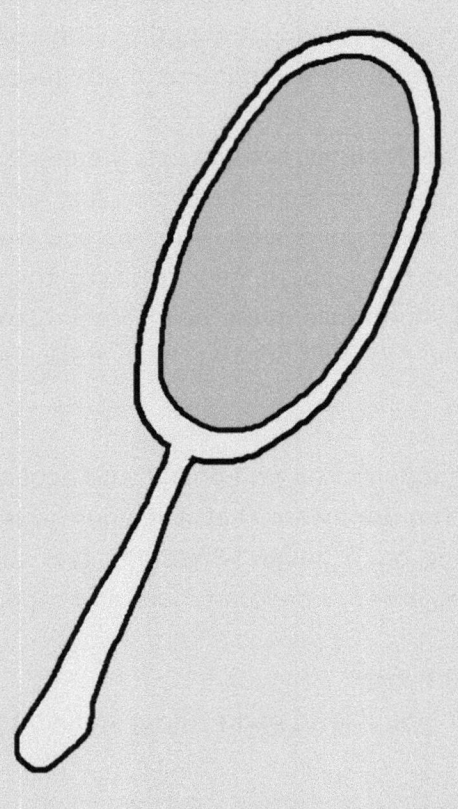

Who are you and who are you not? Your website as a mirror

A website says a lot about the person or the company behind it. I can see for example whether a company thinks customer- and visitor-oriented or not. I can see how much quality lies in that company. Whether it is sure for whom it wants to be here, whether it is friendly, whether it has values. I can feel the character of the company.

But how does it feel when you visit your own website? Do you feel comfortable with it? Do you like yourself when you look into the mirror of your own website? Do you look forward to someone visiting your website and meeting you? Or do you notice elements on your website that no longer suit you? Let them go! Throw your old clothes in the bin and create space for everything that makes you and your company become what it is ultimately all about.

Show yourself in your best version, maybe even the way you see yourself in the near future. A website that truly reflects you and what you offer will strengthen you, while a website that has little to do with you weakens you.

Strengthen the elements that feel like you. Because they make you unique. Your competitors are uninteresting.

Out of one single mould

The magic word of your brand is CONSEQUENCE.

CONSEQUENCE in your thoughts and actions leads to TRUST because your visitor or customer can rely on you. You always behave as your visitor expects you to. For example, you are always friendly, always attentive, always customer-oriented. This is how trust develops over time.

In your company, consistency leads to CHARACTER. You can rely on yourself. You know who you are and you know your values. A strong character also brings charisma.

Ideally everything fits together: your colors, your message, your words, your photos, your videos. The more everything comes together, the more convincing your website will be.

Industry disloyalty:
Leave conventions behind

Often companies are too busy with their competitors. That is why many company websites look very similar. This is boring and not much fun at all. Mark Twain put it this way: „Comparison is the death of joy." In the businesses of the 21st century (constant) comparison is also the death of real success.

Why should we act the way others in our industry do? Why should our website look like the other websites in our industry? By copying we only get lost in the mass of always the same. We should rather stand out! Be noticeable. I designed a website for a tax consultant and my wife contributed some funny comics, like the ones in this book. Suddenly the website stood out and became noticeable among all those serious websites of the other accountants in town. „So the website of a tax consultant can also be fun," the visitor thinks. „Maybe even the time I spend with a tax consultant can be fun." So he chooses the tax consultant that seems more likeable and human than the other ones. My client's website with the comics has been reliably bringing new clients every month for several years now.

You sell cars, but your website doesn't look like a typical car workshop? Perfect! Show the world what you stand for. You sell insurances, but your website doesn't look like a typical insurance company? Great! What is your point of view regarding your industry, your product, your visitors? What do you want to convey to them? Why did you become an entrepreneur in the first place? Be yourself. And show that confidence on your website!

A good website is like a bikini

Boundaries are powerful. They give a profile and make you more attractive. Less is more, but it must not be too little either, because minimalism is not an end in itself.

A good website is like a bikini. Little fabric, high impact.

Formulate short, concise sentences and texts. Design a new subpage only when your visitor really needs it. Use a lot of white space. One often tends to produce too much content over time and forget to delete content that no longer fits one's needs.

Learn to say NO! To unnecessary words, sentences, paragraphs, to unnecessary subpages and elements. Be brave and let go of elements and content over and over again. You will be surprised how well your website will still look afterwards. Even better most of the time. Sometimes it is worth being radical. Can you manage to reduce a page of text to three sentences?

Letting go of elements and content is not always easy, but it's worth it. Because if you leave out unimportant elements, you can put the really important elements in a much better light.

Create attractive bikini websites and bikini content!

An awesome website automatically brings visitors via Google

In this book I have deliberately not written about how to attract visitors. Because it is explicitly about building a convincing website. But I can tell you here and now: If your website is great, your visitors will find you in Google.

If you have implemented the thoughts and impulses in this book, then that means
- You know who your visitor is.
- You know what she wants and needs on your website.
- You know what words she uses.
- You have built content that is important for your visitor, that she likes and that solves her problems.
- You give her a good feeling on your website.
- Your website is linked to other websites because your content is so valuable.

Google then understands that your website is relevant and useful. For example, because your visitors stay on your site for a long time, because there are few dropouts, and because your site is linked on many other sites and in social media.

It's Google's job to objectively assess all of this, and the company has spent years developing an intelligent algorithm for this. Build a great website and Google will send you matching visitors for free. Cool, isn't it?

Your website is a place for your vision of paradise

How would your website look like in a perfect world? Write down what would be important to you, what would be beautiful in your world.

My utopian world looks like this, for example:
- My customers are appreciative and friendly.
- I have interesting encounters and relationships in the exchange with my customers.
- My work gives me energy every day.
- My business is simple and easy.
- My services and products are profitable and bring joy to me and my customers at the same time.
- (...)

Now think about how you stand up for your vision on your website. For example by thinking about how friendly people communicate with each other. And then this is how you communicate. Think about which pictures and colors would resonate with your vision. Maybe it's little images or words, which you can fill with your vision in an unobtrusive way.

Make a choice for your website to make your vision ever more feelable and you will automatically attract all the customers and partners that fit best with you. Your working life will become more and more beautiful. Dream a bit and make your website become this dream, that you are yearning for.

Empathy, the turnkey

The one who can put himself in the position of his visitor best has a decisive advantage. Empathy is a key skill. I perceive the feelings, the needs etc. of my visitor and connect with them. How does my blog post reach my reader? Is she happy? Does she regard the thoughts as useful?

In order to empathize with others, you should practice - like all other skills in life - your empathy. I recommend you to change your perspective frequently. Not only when you work on your website, but also in your everyday life. When you have a fight with someone. When someone behaves differently to what you expected. In a conversation with your customer.

Many things change when you empathize with others. You gain completely new insights and make different, better decisions.

If you find it difficult to empathize with others, I have a little special recommendation: Just choose yourself as the target group. Many successful entrepreneurs went this way.

How do you act and communicate if you don't need money or attention?

Many people are constantly afraid of not having or being enough. I have seen people on stage that are very successful financially who carry a deep sense of lack with them and are so hungry to sell that it hurts my soul. Such people have little faith in life, in abundance and in themselves and their business. The belief „I am and have not enough" seems to be unquestionable and they find it very difficult to free themselves from this negative trance.

Apparently some people can be very successful despite this deep sense of lack they are carrying, but is this success fun then? Begging for money with a thousand arguments? And if these people find an audience, then it is often an audience of more beggars, which even reinforces the „I am not enough" feeling within. Khalil Gibran asks the question: „Is not fear of thirst when the well is full, the thirst that is unquenchable?"

Imagine that you don't need any of this. No money, no attention and no affirmation from others. What kind of person would you be? And how happy would people be to come to you? How freely could you act and express yourself? In life as on your website? How freely can you choose who you are, what you do and what you ask for if you are not afraid of lack? And how alive does this make everything you do? How free do the actual values you offer and convey come to light and enrich your counterpart tangibly, if they are not weighed down by a huge gullet begging for love and money as a reward?

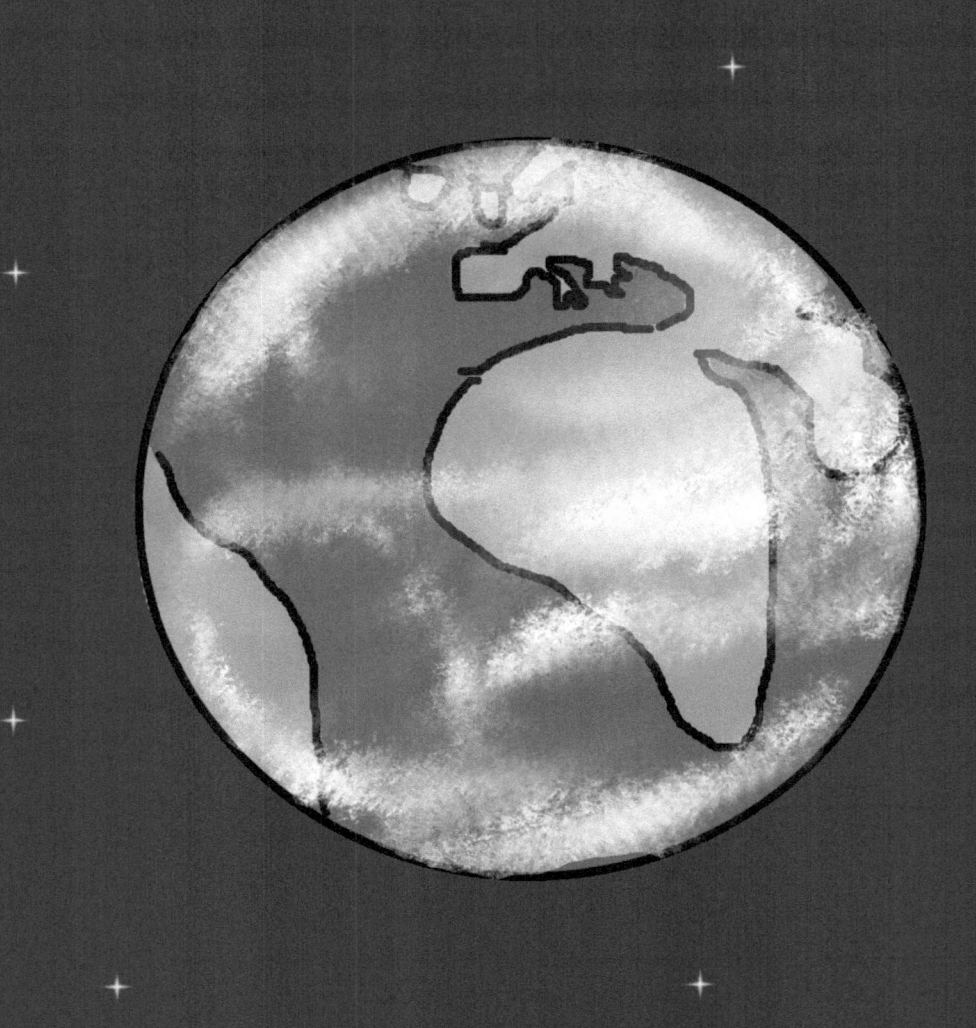

Your potential million people audience

Have you ever realized that the whole world can visit your website? That you are a global player?

Let's assume you only have 300 website visitors per month. This results in 3600 visitors per year and 36000 visitors in ten years. That is a whole stadium full of people. 36000 people who want to meet you and get to know you and what you offer.

It is not about the size of your audience. With just a few encounters you can already make a difference in the world.

But you can access your innate powers and sharpen your senses through the realisation that you have a huge audience. Connect with this potential and your website will become better. Because a lot is at stake. Because you are important. You can't afford to oversleep your performance or be badly prepared. Now is your moment. Now you can show who you are and what you have to offer. Now you can make a difference in the life of people.

Be visible! Be great!

Your beliefs determine what you create

Your website is the result of many decisions. These decisions are determined by your beliefs. Not only your website, but also your company and your world are a reflection of these beliefs and the stories and ideas you tell yourself.

You can change your beliefs. Piece by piece. You have the inward space to move a bit. Developing new beliefs does not mean to run blindly and naively into the fire, but to seize the chances to enter a new world. If you believe something else, you experience another world. With new possibilities.

- What do you believe in?
- What do you want to believe in?
- What positive and alive new belief could you approach?
- Which belief is it time to change?

Your company can be anything you want. You can take unusual paths. Live an exciting life full of adventure. You can make the things you feel and hope inside become your reality. You can get more aligned and in tune with the sounds of your soul.

We believe. We decide. We act. We create. I am curious to see what kind of website you create and how it changes your business.

THANK YOU

Jakob Bantleon
Thank you Jakob, for your refreshing and strengthening energy.

Marc Loskill
Thank you Marc, for setting the book.

Susanne Schmöller
Thank you dearest Susanne, for your wonderful pictures.

Daniel Tietz
Thank you Daniel, for your creativity and inspiration.

My thanks also go to the following people who have contributed to the book in the background through their inspiration:

Günter Faltin
Jason Fried
Seth Godin
David Heinemeier Hansson

Ricarda Kiel
Stefan Merath
Derek Sivers
Ryan Holiday

© Mach DAS Verlag, Markus Bühler
Aufhauser Str. 17/1
73312 Geislingen

www.mach-das.de

Production: BoD - Books on Demand, Norderstedt

ISBN: 978-3-96923-000-8

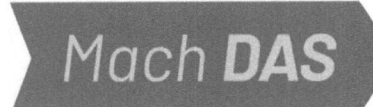